Wildlife of the Town

Guilhem Lesaffre

Illustrations
François Desbordes
and
Jean Chevallier
Claire Felloni
Jean-Michel Kacédan
Alban Larousse
Dominique Mansion
Pascal Robin

Translated by
Josephine Weightman

HarperCollins*Publishers*

COLLINS WATCH GUIDES

Illustrations: Frédéric Denhez
Black and white artwork: Alban Larousse
Translation: Josephine Weightman

ISBN 0 00 220091 0

Printed in Italy

● The **house martin** is the most widespread of the swallow family in towns. It likes to nest under balconies, eaves and ornamental moulding.

● In some towns, the **black-headed gull** has become almost as trusting as the urban pigeon, especially in winter.

● Small rodents like the **house mouse** easily find enough to eat even on underground railway lines.

● In winter, the **moorhen** of northern towns is often forced off the open water when the surface is covered with ice.

● A row of trees is sufficient for the magpie to build its domed nest.

● The **beech marten**, a small non-British carnivore adapted to life in towns, feeds in part on mice and young rats which occupy the same habitat.

● The **fox** is the largest urban wild mammal.

● The **fox** is hardly ever seen in daylight in towns.

Street trees provide birds with somewhere to perch, food and nesting places. They are used as roosts for sparrows, greenfinches and starlings.

● In towns, open water (ornamental pools in town squares or lakes in parks) is full of fish put there as a public amenity. **Carp** is very often the fish chosen for stocking.

● Rivers and canals flowing through towns attract seagulls.

● Below the surface, a range of fish lead silent lives. They are the prey of fish-eating birds like the heron and kingfisher.

● Chimneys and aerials on rooftops are attractive to birds as they are well away from the bustle and noise of the streets.

● Historic buildings are safe places for birds like the **jackdaw**, **owl** and **swift**. Mammals use them too - bats find plenty of shelter among the old stones or among the timbers where it is dark

● The **martin's** nest is made of mud and is enclosed, with an opening at the top.

Swallow's nest

● The **swallow** has a red breast and rather chestnut under-parts. It has a black back and a long, forked tail.

Swifts and Swallows

Swifts and swallows only enliven urban skies during the summer months. Once the nesting period is over, these great travellers return to Africa. This is where they spend the winter, still hunting the flying insects which form their only food. Swifts swoop through the air screaming. They depart very early, at the end of July.

● The **swift** nests in colonies in holes in buildings. It spends most of its time flying, landing only for nest building, egg laying and feeding its young. Young birds may fly for two years before they nest.

● Eaves of buildings also provide many nest sites.

● Material for building the nest is picked up while the bird is flying. In this way, the swift gathers wisps of straw, blades of grass and hair or fur carried along by air currents.

● The **swift** does not need to land in order to drink. It merely raises its wings and brushes the surface of the water with its beak.

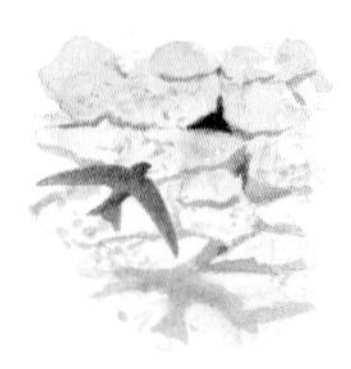

● **Swifts** use crevices in walls as nest sites.

Rats and Mice

House mouse

A vast number of small rodents have found it possible to live in towns. Food and places to hide away are plentiful and predators are not very numerous. Man, although a sworn enemy to rats and mice – more to be feared than cats, beech martens and foxes – has not been able to eliminate them.

● The **brown rat** loves water, even dirty water. It is an excellent swimmer, and unafraid of crossing a water way. But to invade islands, large and small, it usually travels in the hold of ships. After being in the water it dries its thick fur by sleeking it down.

● **Rats** have been able to adapt very easily to the most modern towns.

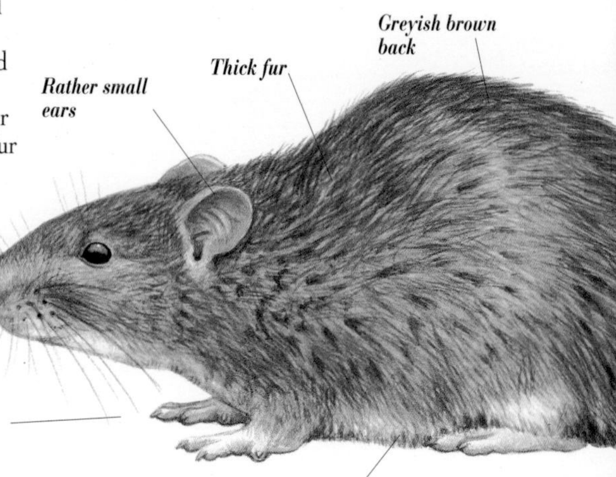

● Town rodents take advantage of what man unwittingly puts at their disposal. Everything is good to eat to a rat, even the least appetising scraps.

● The **brown rat** can be identified by its brown fur and by its ears which are smaller than those of its cousin, the black rat.

The black rat has been pushed out by the larger and more aggressive brown rat in most areas. It is more likely to be found in lofts than in cellars or sewers, but is now very rare in Britain.

● **Droppings** are often the only indication of the presence of rodents.

Rat

Mouse

● Rat droppings are a good centimetre long while mouse droppings are 6–7mm.

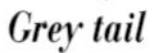

Grey tail

● The **house mouse** is distinctly smaller than the rat (300–500g), weighing between 12 and 22g.

House mouse: entirely grey

● Female **brown rats** are able to reproduce at three months and may give birth to young every seven to eight weeks, hence the abundance of these creatures in our towns.

● Mice are rather more fussy in what they eat. Given a choice, they prefer seeds, but have been known to nibble at inedible objects!

● An apple core lends some variety to the menu. The pips are enjoyed as much as the flesh. Seeds that have fallen out of a bag are quickly picked up as a delicacy.

Short sparse hairs

Tail shorter than that of the black rat

The tail is useful for balancing

● A piece of dry bread provides a real feast for rodents. In a way, these animals help clear up rubbish.

Back foot

Front foot

● In mud or dust, it is possible to pick out tracks left by rats and mice. Prints left by the house mouse are similar to those of the rat, but smaller.

● **Rat footprints**. Front foot: four toes well spread out, with claws. Hind foot: five toes, one shorter and clearly separate from the others.

Seagulls

Seagulls have become regular visitors to many towns in the winter months. They do not fear man and have become as bold as pigeons. These water birds feed at rubbish dumps as well as along rivers and canals. They take small fish and all manner of scraps carried along by the current.

● **Gulls** are adept at picking up food from the surface of the water.

● The **herring gull** has a wingspan of 1.5m. The black-headed gull is smaller with a wingspan of less than a metre.

● In winter the head of the **black-headed gull** turns white, apart from a round patch behind the eye. In spring, the breeding colours include a black cap.

● There are brown patches in the plumage of juvenile **black-headed gulls**.

● For some years **herring gulls** have been boldly building their nests on roofs and chimneys in towns, especially seaside towns.

Common gull

The common gull is smaller than the herring gull and frequents rivers and open water in the towns of northern Europe. In the winter, it moves down into Western Europe.

● All sorts of building materials are used by urban gulls: odd lengths of string, bits of plastic bag etc

The herring gull's massive beak is designed for cutting

Juvenile herring gull

Primary feathers with white spots

● **Juvenile herring gulls** have uniformly grey-brown plumage, apart from the white tail with a black band at the end.

● The **black-headed gull**, which is the most urban of the gulls, has been overwintering in towns since the turn of the century, attracted by the large rubbish tips.

Pigeons and Doves

Pigeons and collared doves are among the birds best adapted to life in towns. Sometimes there are so many of the former that their number has to be controlled. In Paris there used to be 200,000 rock doves, four times as many as now.

● The **stock dove** sometimes perches on historic buildings and statues which it fouls with its droppings.

● The **domestic pigeon** is a variety of the rock dove which lives on cliffs in the wild. Its plumage varies widely.

● The **stock dove** can be recognised by its wholly grey plumage and dark eye. It nests in hollow trees or cavities in stone walls.

● The **collared dove** began to invade Europe from Asia in the first half of the 20th century. Nowadays it is found everywhere and is even colonising North Africa.

● The **woodpigeon** is the largest of this group of birds. It is easily distinguished from its cousins by the white neck patch and the white bar on its wing. Its nest is built from twigs in the fork of a tree.

● When winter ends, the **woodpigeon** displays and can be heard cooing. Soon the male can be seen bringing twigs into the tree where it has built a nest.

Pigeons and doves are the only birds which can drink water from a fountain with a sucking action

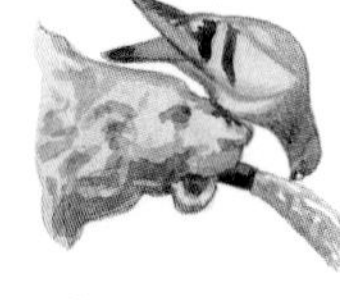

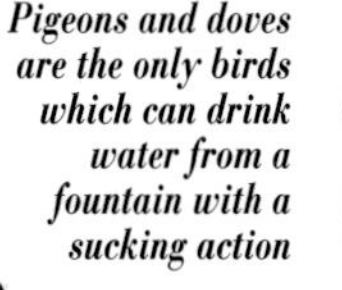

● The **woodpigeon** displays by soaring up, clattering its wings then gliding down.

● Pigeons and turtle doves find some of their food on the ground in the form of crumbs and seeds. In spring, they also eat the buds and young shoots of trees.

Foxes and Beech Martens

The beech marten, a non-British species, and the fox are visitors to towns. These carnivores, which are attracted in the first place by easily available scraps, are not slow to take to foraging in dustbins. However, they are usually unobtrusive and difficult to spot.

Paw print of the beech marten

● The print has five digits.

Short ears and pointed muzzle

● The **beech marten** has a supple body and long furry tail. Its white bib gives it away as it steals along in the darkness.

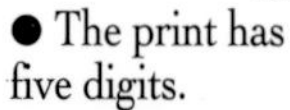

● The **beech marten** is as much at ease in towns as a cat. It is only active at night and therefore mostly passes unnoticed.

Dog

● The paw print of a dog is wide with the claws fanning out.

Fox

● The **paw print** of a fox is similar to a dog's but the claws all point forward and a line can be drawn between the pads.

Roofs form part of the territory of the urban beech marten

● The **fox** has lived in towns for 40 years. It has taken, in particular, to the suburbs, coming out to forage at nightfall.

● The **fox** leaps upon the rodent he has spotted.

● The **young foxes** wait at the earth for the adult to bring back a catch.

Fox droppings are often tapered at one end

● The beech marten and fox eat scraps of food, fruit and anything small they can catch. The fox is very keen on earthworms.

● The beech marten's **droppings** are more distinctive than the fox's which often look like those of a dog.

● Cherry stones are often found in the dung of these two carnivores.

● It is not easy to find the **tracks of a fox** in town. In winter, after a fall of snow, you may be able to see its prints.

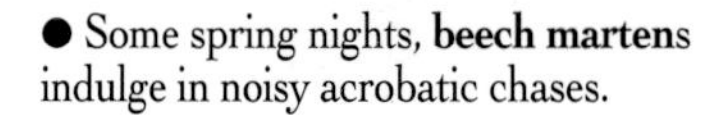

● Some spring nights, **beech martens** indulge in noisy acrobatic chases.

Butterflies

As soon as the first fine days arrive, butterflies bring small touches of colour to our towns. They are mostly found in parks and gardens but also fly up and down the streets going from window box to flower pot. They do not all hatch out in towns as the food plant necessary for the caterpillar may not grow there.

● The chrysalis of the **peacock butterfly** looks like a leaf. Inside, the caterpillar turns into a butterfly.

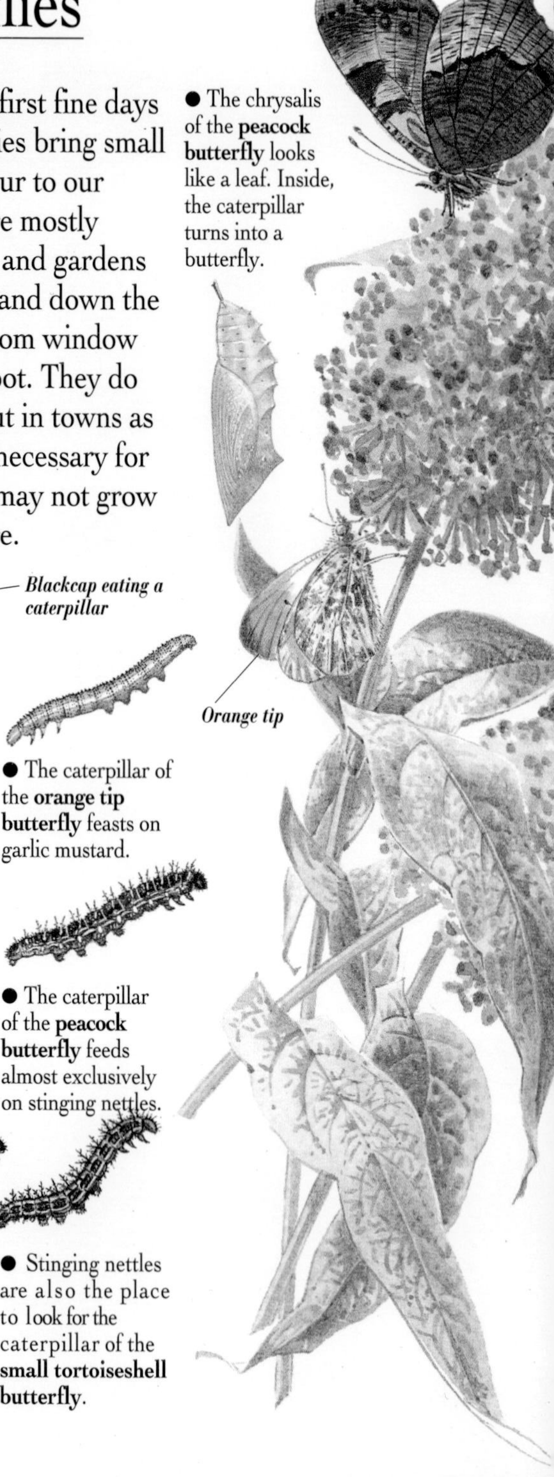

● Insect-eating birds search for the plump caterpillars which are very nutritious.

● The caterpillar of the **orange tip butterfly** feasts on garlic mustard.

● **Bees** and **bumblebees** seek out pollen and nectar from flowers in the towns.

● The caterpillar of the **peacock butterfly** feeds almost exclusively on stinging nettles.

● The caterpillar of the **painted lady butterfly** feeds on stinging nettles, thistles, mallow and burdock.

● Stinging nettles are also the place to look for the caterpillar of the **small tortoiseshell butterfly**.

● The **painted lady butterfly** is not very common in towns. However, you may see it from March or April until October. It is a migratory species which flies north in summer as the days get warmer.

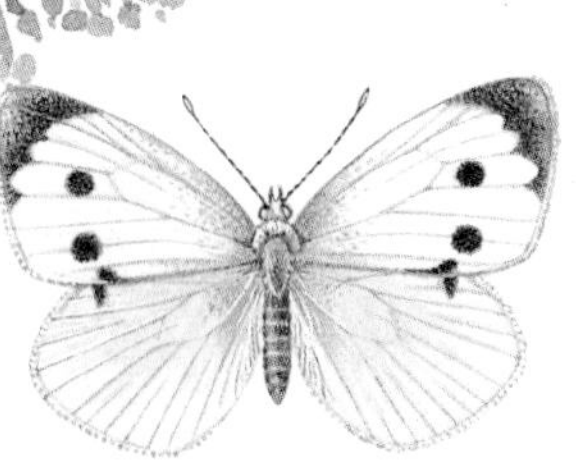

● The **cabbage white butterfly** is one of the most common urban butterflies. The wing markings vary according to sex and season.

● The flowering spikes of the **buddleia,** a shrub originating in China, attract butterflies all summer thanks to their abundant nectar.

● The splendid colouring of the **small tortoiseshell butterfly** disappears when the insect closes its wings. Then its camouflage is perfect.

● Patches of wasteland often support plants popular with butterflies and their caterpillars.

● The **peacock butterfly** is one of the most beautiful found in towns. It overwinters in a sheltered place, and flies as soon as the sun comes out in spring.

The Kestrel

The kestrel is a reminder to town dwellers of how enterprising nature is. This small raptor is one of the best adapted to life in our cities. It nests on ancient monuments or tall buildings and has even taken to modern tower blocks from which it hunts.

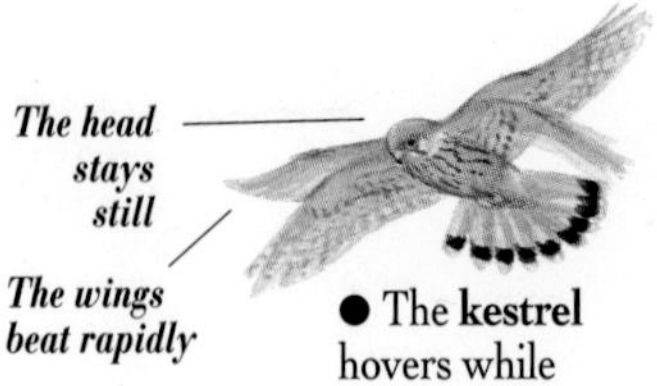

The head stays still

The wings beat rapidly

● The **kestrel** hovers while seeking its prey which it can locate from a great height as it has very sharp eyesight.

● Once it has located its prey, the raptor dives with its wings half closed.

Male

Female

The peregrine falcon sometimes becomes established in towns, feeding on pigeons and jackdaws.

● The male **kestrel** is 40cm long, has a grey head, speckled red-brown back and grey tail with a black bar at the end. The female is less colourful than the male; the tail is brown and the head does not have a grey cap.

● As it lands, it thrusts forward its sharp talons.

Another urban raptor is the tawny owl which preys on sleeping sparrows.

● Urban kestrels catch sparrows and mice as well as large insects. They even sometimes catch lizards.

● Its **pellets** contain the indigestible parts of its prey: feathers, fur and bones.

● The **young** remain huddled together under cover for about four weeks before risking their first flight.

● Between hunting flights, the **kestrel** likes to sit on a favourite post.

● Historic buildings provide **kestrels** with many nest sites as well as numerous resting places.

● The **kestrel** soars with tail and wings spread, taking advantage of air currents. It takes little effort.

Garden Birds

In the autumn, most blackcaps leave the gardens of European towns to winter in Africa.

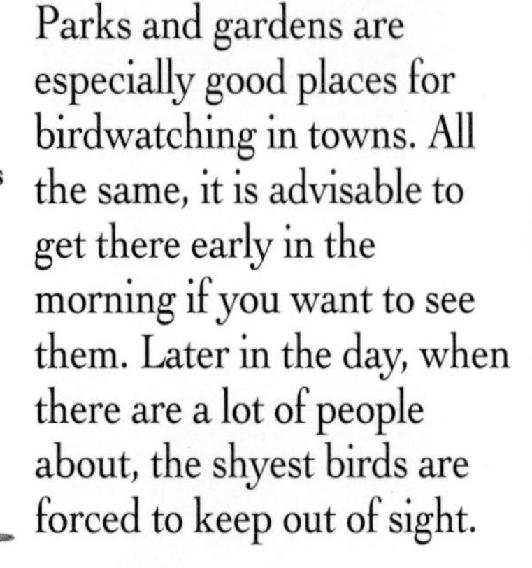

Parks and gardens are especially good places for birdwatching in towns. All the same, it is advisable to get there early in the morning if you want to see them. Later in the day, when there are a lot of people about, the shyest birds are forced to keep out of sight.

● The **nuthatch** nests in a hole in a tree, reducing the size of the opening with mud.

● The **jay,** which has blue flashes on its wings, is usually a woodland bird. However, it has learnt how to live comfortably in many parks.

● The **robin's** nest, which is often rather low down, may be destroyed by cats.

Small size but powerful song

● The **spotted flycatcher** watches from its post for an insect to fly past. After the catch, it returns to its post.

● The **greenfinch** feeds exclusively on seeds. It has a strong conical beak with which it breaks open the seed coat.

● A park must be sufficiently bushy and not have too many stray cats in order for the tiny wren to move in.

Greenfinches are happy to drink at bird tables

● The **goldcrest,** one of the smallest garden birds, is mostly found in conifers.

● When alarmed, the **magpie** flicks its long tail.

● Sometimes the **magpie** goes for the eggs of small song birds but its own nest is robbed by the crow, which is a larger bird.

Sparrows

Young house sparrow

The house sparrow, which occurs more or less everywhere in the world, is the bird of towns and villages that everyone recognises. It has become man's inseparable companion and very largely depends on him. This bird, restless and resourceful, can seize any opportunity to find food and build its nest.

- The young **house sparrow** looks very like the female. It can be distinguished by yellow corners at the base of the beak which give it a rather sulky look. This thickened skin disappears when the bird is adult.

- The **sparrow** can catch insects while in the air. It can hover like a hummingbird.

- The **sparrow** lives in groups. There may be several hundred birds in one roost, possibly thousands.

- When the birds are pairing off, there are frequent rows and domestic scenes.

Faced with three males courting her, the female sparrow is on the defensive

The tree sparrow, a bird of the countryside, is much rarer than the town sparrow. It has a brown crown.

The dunnock is often confused with the sparrow, but it has the slender pointed beak of the insect eater.

● The **house sparrow** has learnt to profit from our rubbish and even frequents litter bins.

● A good **dust bath** helps in the fight against parasites living among the feathers.

● The female sparrow has dull, predominantly beige plumage.

● **Sparrows' nests** are usually in a hole: a gap in a wall, under a roof, lamp-post or air vent. The female lines her nest with feathers and blades of grass, then lays five or six eggs which she sits on for about two weeks.

● When flying, the sparrow can be recognised by its short squat silhouette, its rapid flight and the way it glides down to earth.

● The young leave the downy nest after two weeks. They are fed on insects and larvae, then softened seeds.

● The sparrow's menu includes seeds and crumbs. In spring, it also eats buds and insects.

● In spring, the male sports very white cheeks and a broad black bib.

Blackbirds and Starlings

● **Blackbirds** often choose very strange places to nest as here, for instance, in the rim of a wheel.

Blackbirds are popular in towns as they have a melodious song but starlings can be be a nuisance when they become too numerous.
Under their roosts in trees, pavements, vehicles and unlucky passers-by can be fouled by their droppings.

● The **male blackbird** is wholly black apart from the beak and pretty yellow eye rim. The female has brownish plumage.

● With the autumn, the starling exchanges its black plumage with a metallic gloss for one with white speckles.

● When it makes its harsh call or its mimicking calls, the **male starling** ruffles its feathers and flutters its wings.

White blackbird: this is a blackbird lacking pigment in all its plumage

Fieldfare

The colourful fieldfare is common in towns of northern and eastern Europe.

Song thrush

The song thrush is a virtuoso performer whose song rings out once winter has ended.

● The **blackbird** chooses a song post somewhere high up. This accomplished soloist makes use of chimney pots and television aerials.

● The **blackbird** is expert at catching worms. Once the prey is located, it is pulled out without further ado.

● On the ground, the blackbird hops along in a hurry. It also runs for short distances.

● The **starling's** jaunty walk distinguishes it from the blackbird, even at a distance.

The starling has a much shorter tail than the blackbird

Water Birds

Lakes and large ornamental ponds attract a range of aquatic birds. Some are nesting birds, others only over-winter. Most have become used to people and are not frightened if approached.

● As large as your fist, the **little grebe** sports its more brightly coloured breeding plumage in spring.

● The **kingfisher** is one of the most beautiful birds that can be seen along the bank beside open water. It darts along the water's edge.

● The **grey wagtail** spends the winter over lakes and rivers in towns. It flies up and down the banks, nimbly catching tiny insects that it swallows whole.

Grey wagtail

● A **cygnet** can be recognised by its pinkish beak and grey-brown plumage.

● A **swan** in flight is always an impressive sight.

● The adult **mute swan** has a knob at the base of its beak.

● The **tufted duck** is a small diving duck. The male has a distinct crest on the back of its head.

● The **moorhen** constantly flicks its tail revealing the white part underneath.

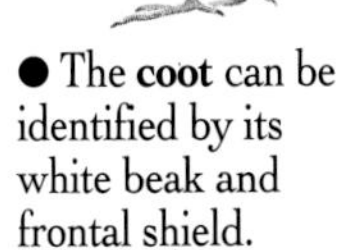

● The **coot** can be identified by its white beak and frontal shield.

● The **mallard** is the most widespread of urban ducks. The female is camouflaged on her nest by her plumage.

Coot

Wings raised, two coots challenge each other

Birds which dabble for food remain on the surface while 'divers' can swim underwater and so are able to feed on the bottom.

Spiders and Ladybirds

Among clumps of flowers, bushes and curtains of ivy live fearful miniature hunters. Often unnoticed by passers-by, they are nonetheless lying in wait. Spiders prefer to lspin their webs and put their faith in patience. Ladybirds, on the other hand, have opted for a life of action. Flies and aphids fall victim to these little predators.

Small abdomen (male)

Rounded abdomen (female)

● The cross of white spots is visible on the upper side of the abdomen.

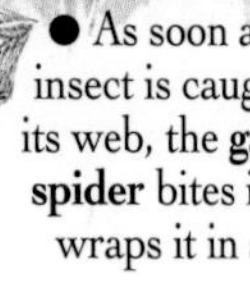

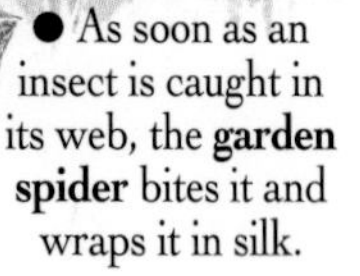

Garden spider

● As soon as an insect is caught in its web, the **garden spider** bites it and wraps it in silk.

● The **garden spider** chooses good supports for its trap.

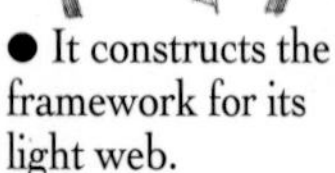

● It constructs the framework for its light web.

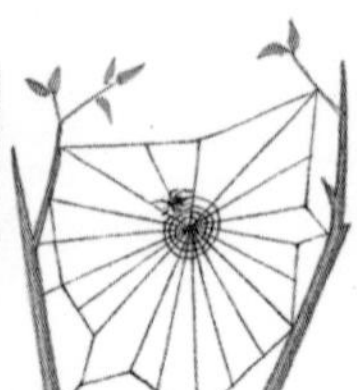

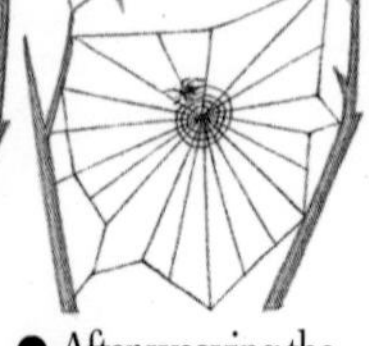

● After weaving the radiating threads, it joins them up.

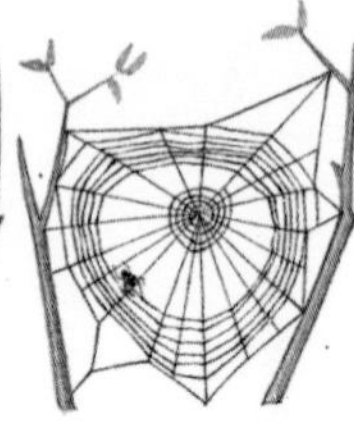

● The web will soon be ready for action.

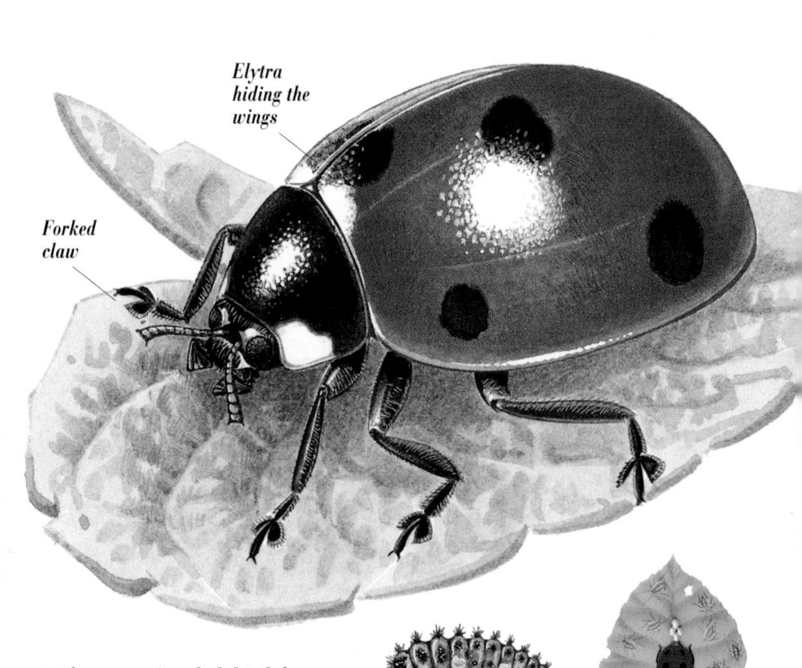

● The **seven-spot ladybird** destroys large numbers of aphids, those tiny insects so hated by gardeners. In some towns, ladybirds are even more popular than chemical products in the battle against aphids.

● **Ladybird larvae** also have black spots.

The female lays her eggs on a leaf that aphids have invaded. As soon as they hatch, the hungry larvae make quickly for the aphids and devour them.

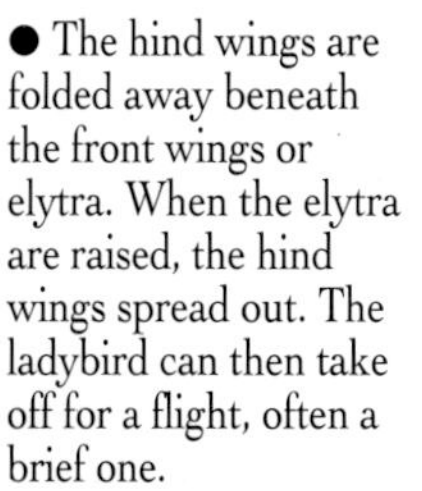

● The hind wings are folded away beneath the front wings or elytra. When the elytra are raised, the hind wings spread out. The ladybird can then take off for a flight, often a brief one.

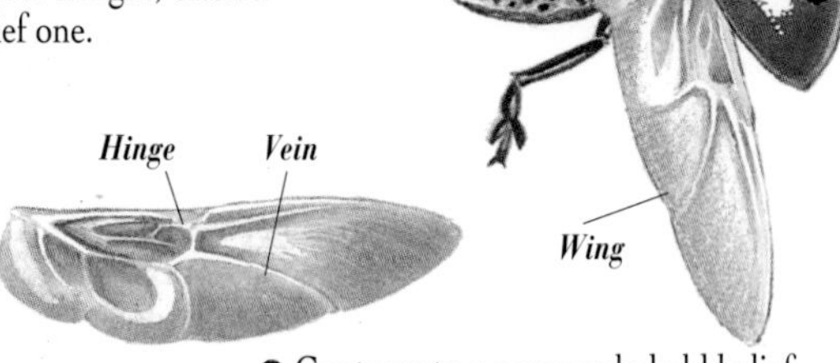

● Contrary to a commonly held belief, the spots on a ladybird do not indicate age but species. There can be as many as 24 spots.

● The transparent **wing** has a hinge and can close like the blade of a penknife.

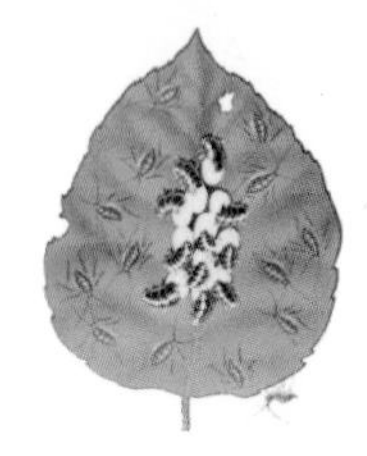

Bats

All through the summer months, bats have the freedom of the night skies in towns. Several species of these small winged mammals swoop over roof tops and up and down streets. They can be seen hunting the insects attracted to street lights.

● **Daubenton's bat** hunts insects over open water in parks. In the summer, it roosts in hollow trees or lofts. In the winter, it roosts in caves.

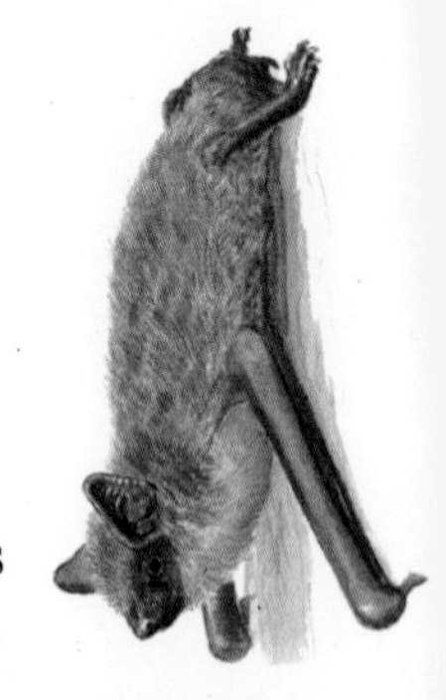

● The **serotine** can be seen right in the centre of towns and only emerges just before nightfall. It hibernates from October to April in cellars, caves or old lofts.

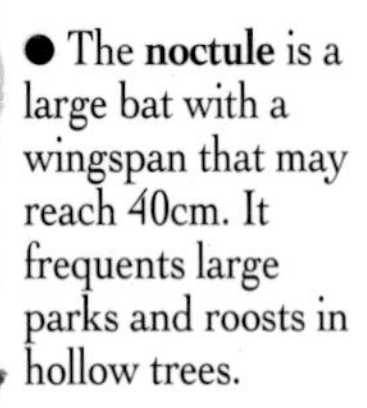

● The **noctule** is a large bat with a wingspan that may reach 40cm. It frequents large parks and roosts in hollow trees.

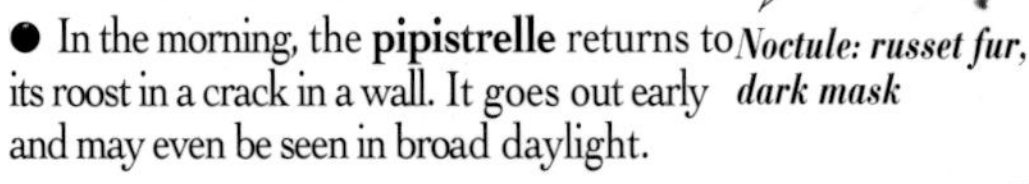

● In the morning, the **pipistrelle** returns to its roost in a crack in a wall. It goes out early and may even be seen in broad daylight.

Noctule: russet fur, dark mask

● The bat utters high pitched squeaks which echo off obstacles. It locates its prey by picking up these echoes. The bat uses this sonar to find its way in the dark.

● The free thumb has a claw and helps the **pipistrelle** to hang on to irregularities on vertical surfaces.

● The **pipistrelle** likes to spend daylight hours behind shutters.

Craneflies are taken by daubenton's bat. The very large old lady moth would be a choice catch. Bats consume very many night-flying moths and other insects.

Crane fly

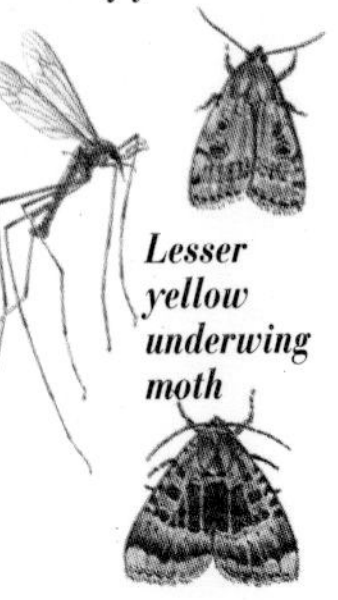

Lesser yellow underwing moth

Old lady moth

Fish

Rivers, canals and other areas of open water in towns support an unexpected variety of fish. Efforts made to improve the quality of water have been successful and fishermen have returned. However, accidents can still cause pollution.

● The lower fins of the **chub** are orange and its silvery sides often have a golden shimmer. This is a fish which tolerates water of poor quality.

The trout jumps to swallow a mosquito

Chub: orange lower fins

● The **cat fish**, which comes from North America, was introduced into Europe in 1885. It is a bottom dweller and is active at night.

● The **zander** is a voracious predator which may measure more than a metre in length. It does not hunt by lying in ambush among plants but openly tracks down small fish.

Zander

Tench

● The **tench** is herbivorous but may also consume larvae, molluscs and worms. During the day, it stays at the bottom.

● The main predatory fish are pike, perch, zander, cat fish and trout. In some rivers, where they have food at their disposal, pike can grow to over one metre in length and weigh about 10 kilos.

● The diet of various fishes includes aquatic plants as well as tadpoles, insects and their larvae, worms or sometimes fry and even adult fish.

● The **gudgeon** and **roach** are eaten by the carnivorous fish living in the rivers.

● Water plants are essential if fish are to reproduce. Without vegetation, the females of some species would have nowhere to attach their eggs which are enveloped in a sticky mucus. The most frequent plants used are the pondweeds, bur-reeds and hornworts.

● In summer, fish may die if the water does not contain enough oxygen.

Studying Urban Wildlife

● The minimum requirement is a book on birds and another on insects.

● With their help you can identify the species you have found and then draw up a list.

Wildlife in towns is investigated in the same way as in the countryside. If you want not only to watch but also to keep records of what you have discovered, it is essential to have some fairly inexpensive basic equipment. A camera is useful but not obligatory.

● A naturalist never goes out without his notebook. It supplies the gaps in his memory and is a mine of important information about sites, dates and species seen.

Notebook: write down the date, the place, conditions, species description, etc

Sketchbook

Somewhere high up, eg a hill or mound, is often a good place for watching migrating birds

Paint box

● Even if you do not have a talent for drawing, it is useful to make a sketch of some species you see (use watercolours, coloured pencils, felt-tips). They help you to remember diagnostic features and to identify more easily what you saw.

● The best dates to watch migrating birds are from late February to early May and from September to November. Dates may, however, vary locally.

● Binoculars are essential for bird watching. Nowadays, a fairly cheap pair will give you satisfactory results. It is important for your comfort to choose a pair that is not too heavy.

A x7 or x8 magnification is ideal

● A hand lens is helpful for identifying small insects.

● A 35mm reflex camera with interchangeable lenses is the most useful.

● If you live in town, you can watch bird migration provided you have a high observation point.

● With a small telephoto lens you can get pictures of birds or mammals. On the other hand, for insects you need a macro lens.

From a high rise tower the visual field is actually limited (you are too high)

The roof of a fairly high block of flats offers an ideal panoramic view

If all else fails, you can do some watching from an attic window

Helping Birds

Provided you have a window ledge, it is easy to help town birds by giving them food and water. However, the food offered must conform with local by-laws which may forbid the feeding of pigeons. A way has to be found so that the food offered is not accessible to these species. It is also possible to encourage birds to nest.

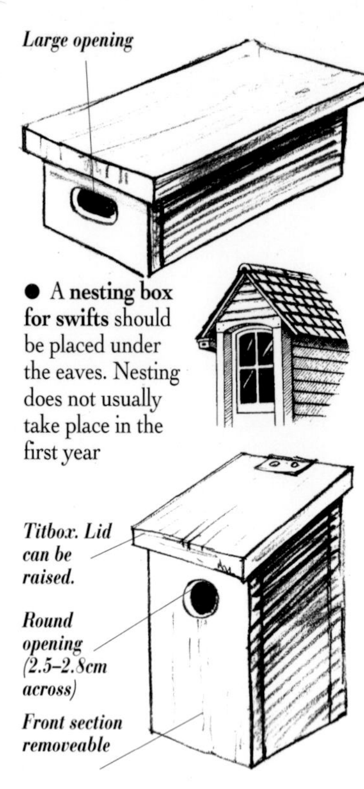

● A **nesting box for swifts** should be placed under the eaves. Nesting does not usually take place in the first year

● A nesting box of this shape is suitable for **great tits** and **blue tits**. It may be sited on a wall or, even better, on a tree trunk in the garden.

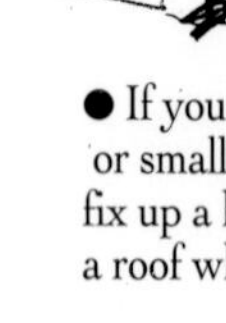

● A **nesting box for house martins** should be fixed under the eaves. It is advisable to fix several together as this increases their attraction.

● If you have a balcony or small garden, you can fix up a hanging **feeder** with a roof which keeps the feed dry.

● You can obtain all models of nesting box from the bird protection societies (see p47 for addresses).

● Seed-eating birds need to drink often. Change their water daily.

● **Sunflower seeds** as well as millet, canary grass and hempseed are much loved by greenfinches and tits.

● Birds may be fed all year round. Never leave out salted nuts. You can make a 'bird soup' of fat and scraps for birds which should prove very popular! Food should always be fresh and, of course, it is essential for you to make sure that cats cannot reach the place you have chosen.

Seasons in Towns

● The **grey heron** can mainly be seen in winter.

Grey heron: flies with its neck pulled back

Even in towns, the effect on wildlife of the changing seasons is perceptible. Trees have a different appearance, one set of birds is replaced by another and insects appear or disappear.

● **Cranes** fly in a large V formation or in long curved lines.

● Their call sounds like a trumpet blast.

The siskin arrives in the autumn

It is easy to watch birds when the trees have lost their leaves

● Birds in parks are different depending on the season. In wintertime, birds fly in from the north.

Swallows hunting insects

Swifts hunting over grassland rich in winged insects. Very rapid flight.

● As the weather improves, migratory birds come back from southern Europe or Africa. Plants burst into leaf and provide a protective screen for tree-loving song birds.

The chiffchaff rhythmically taps out its repetitive call

● During the migration season huge flocks of **woodpigeon** regularly fly over towns in untidy groups.

White bar on the wing

Cranes fly calmly with their necks outstretched

● In autumn or spring a flock of **cranes** in formation may venture over a town. Sometimes these large birds circle round and round.

● On some days, flights of migrating birds pass over in succession.

Greylag geese on migration

● **Wild geese** fly in a V formation or in a line, just like cranes. However they have a faster wing beat than those large waders. The wings are rather short and triangular.

● Towards the end of April, **March-flies** take to the skies in great numbers in many towns. They can easily be recognised by their slow ungainly flight.

Starling

March-fly

● **Starlings** are very busy hunting this easy prey.

Collecting Signs

If you keep your eyes open on natural history walks you can build up a small collection of various objects that indicate an animal has been there. Feathers and shells are some of the clues to pick up. You can also take this opportunity to look for tracks left behind by birds or mammals.

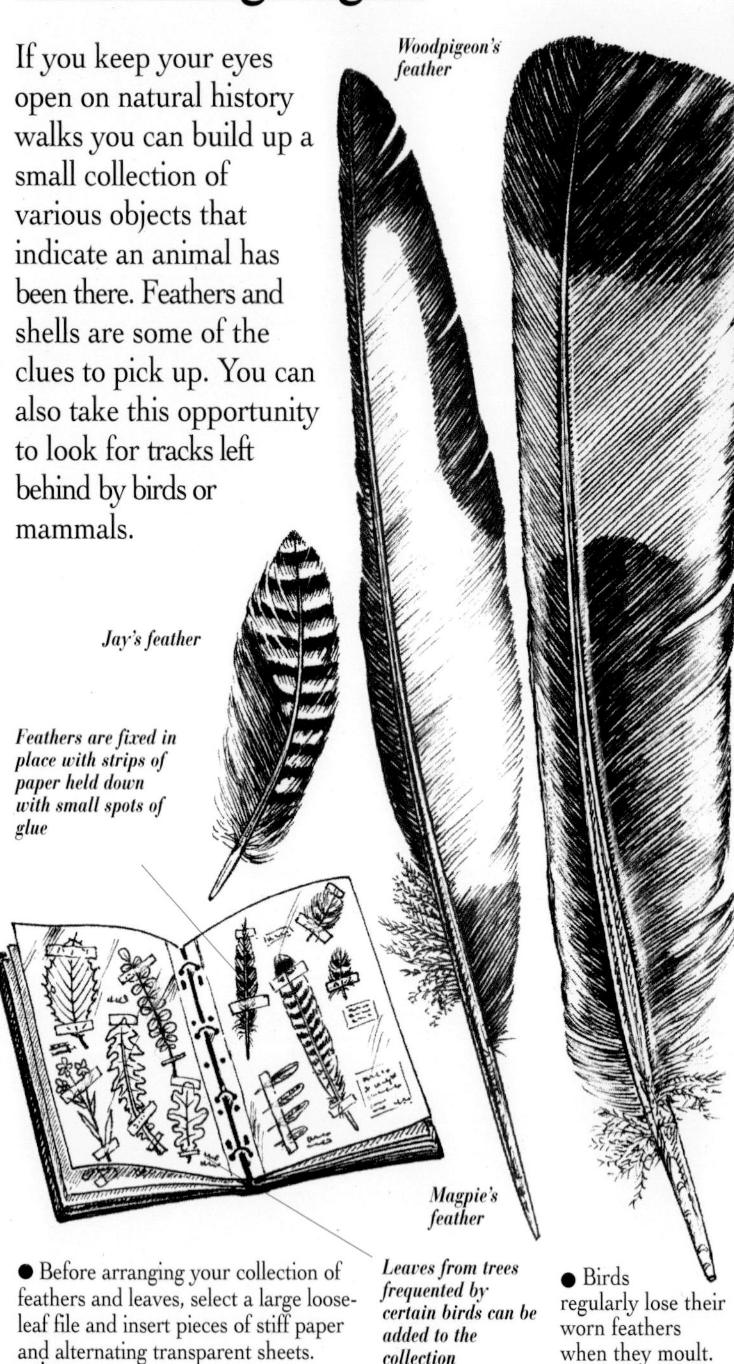

- Before arranging your collection of feathers and leaves, select a large loose-leaf file and insert pieces of stiff paper and alternating transparent sheets.

Leaves from trees frequented by certain birds can be added to the collection

- Birds regularly lose their worn feathers when they moult.

● Always take care to note the date and place you have found various signs.

● Opportunities to detect animal prints are rare in towns. Garden paths and snow may however retain some tracks that can be photographed or sketched.

● All kinds of collections can be kept safely in small boxes: pieces of egg shell or snail shells, dried insects etc.

● Leaves cut by a leaf-cutter bee have characteristic shapes.

● The leaf-cutter bee uses the carefully-cut leaf fragments to make sausage-shaped cells in which she lays her eggs.

● Fragile samples, such as shells or dry insects, are best handled with tweezers.

Trees and Birds

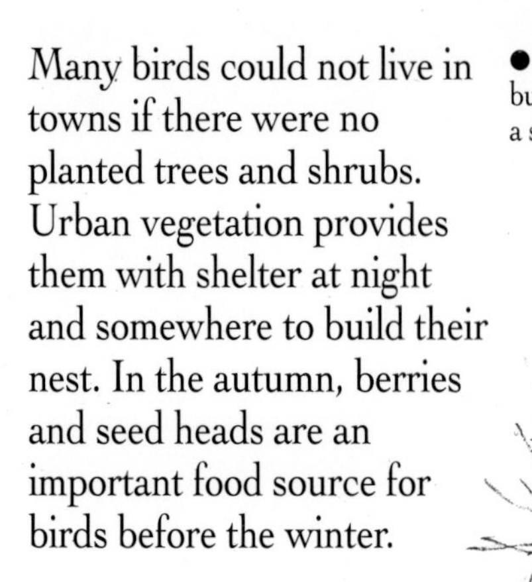

Many birds could not live in towns if there were no planted trees and shrubs. Urban vegetation provides them with shelter at night and somewhere to build their nest. In the autumn, berries and seed heads are an important food source for birds before the winter.

● Birds tend to build their nests at a set height.

A squirrel's ball-shaped drey built on top of an old magpie's nest

● Different birds nest in the same tree: some use branches, others holes in the trunk.

Treecreeper

● Bark dislodged from a tree or a crack is suitable for the **treecreeper**.

From left to right: nests of carrion crow, magpie and woodpigeon

An old woodpecker hole provides a nest site for the great tit

Big holes are occupied by larger birds like the stock dove

● **Conifer cones** yield seeds for the great spotted woodpecker and the squirrel. These birds tear off the scales to get at the seeds.

● The **horse chestnut** welcomes nests. Birds do not eat its fruit.

● **Privet** has black berries if it is not pruned.

● The red berries of **yew** are eaten by many birds, especially the mistle thrush.

● **Lime fruits** are nibbled by chaffinches and greenfinches.

● **Ivy** has blue fruits which ripen in late winter providing food for starving birds.

● Trees and shrubs like the rowan or elder are sometimes covered in thrushes and blackbirds busily gorging the berries.

Food Chains

If there were no available food, the animals inhabiting towns would go away. In urban habitats, as in the wider countryside, food chains link predator and prey. If one of the links is missing, the consequences are felt all along the chain.

● **Great tits** seek food mainly among the branches.

Great tit

● In spring, insects and their larvae form the main part of the diet of great tits, while in winter seeds are very important.

The black-headed gull can feed while still flying

Caterpillar

● While the baby great tits are being reared, each hungry family consumes several hundred **caterpillars** each day.

Stinging nettle

● Stinging nettles are not only 'weeds'. They are the main food source for several species of the caterpillars of butterflies.

● Small fish and fry form part of the diet of the **black-headed gull**.

Fry

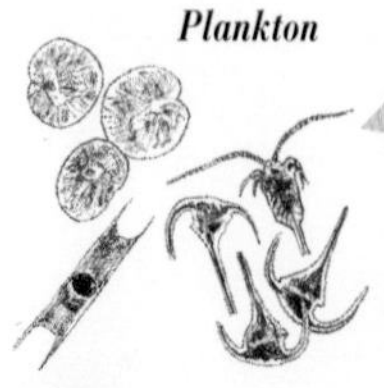

Plankton

● **Plankton** consists of innumerable animal and plant micro-organisms which live suspended in water. It is food for fry and small fish.

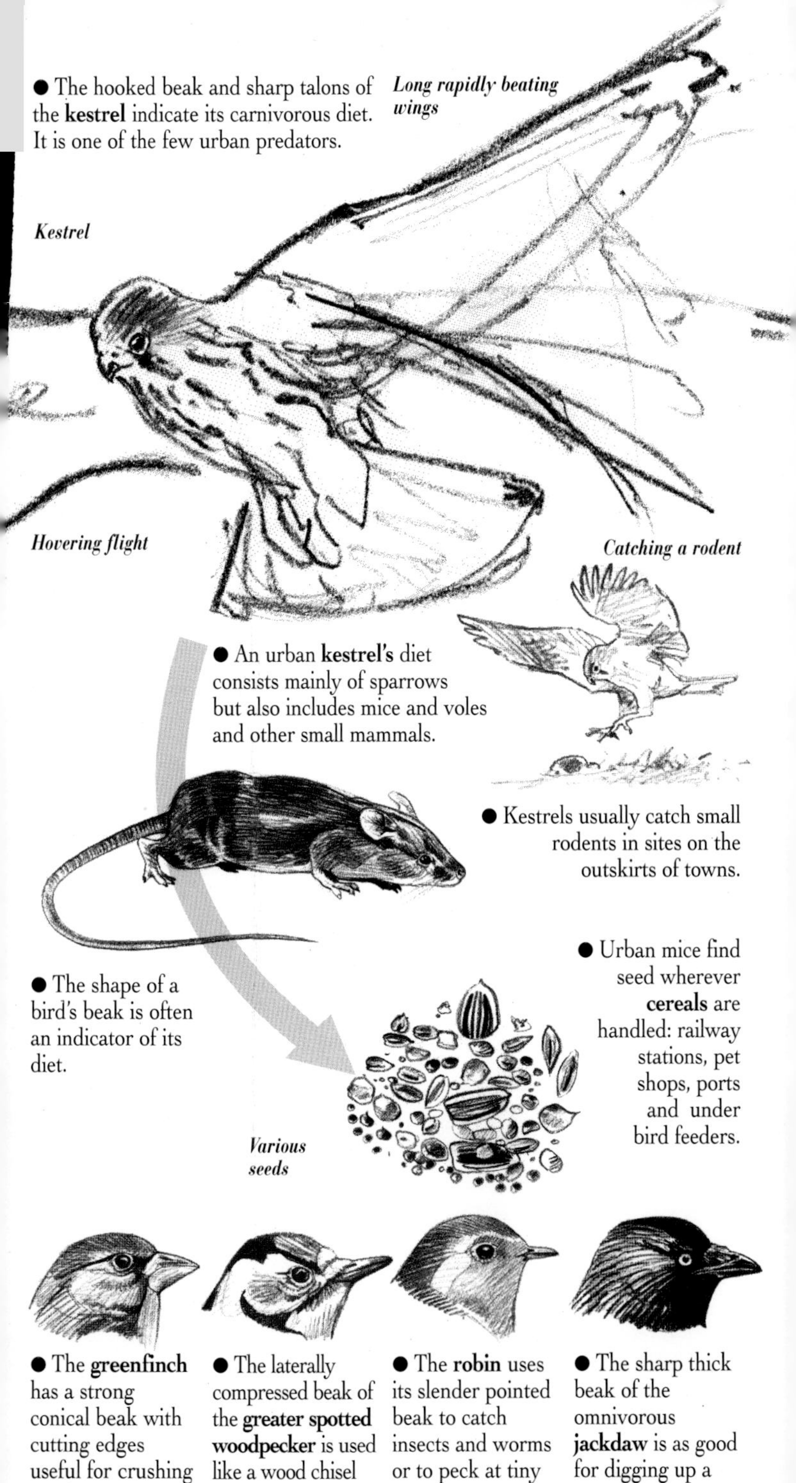

● The hooked beak and sharp talons of the **kestrel** indicate its carnivorous diet. It is one of the few urban predators.

● An urban **kestrel's** diet consists mainly of sparrows but also includes mice and voles and other small mammals.

● Kestrels usually catch small rodents in sites on the outskirts of towns.

● Urban mice find seed wherever **cereals** are handled: railway stations, pet shops, ports and under bird feeders.

● The shape of a bird's beak is often an indicator of its diet.

● The **greenfinch** has a strong conical beak with cutting edges useful for crushing seeds.

● The laterally compressed beak of the **greater spotted woodpecker** is used like a wood chisel to dislodge larvae.

● The **robin** uses its slender pointed beak to catch insects and worms or to peck at tiny seeds.

● The sharp thick beak of the omnivorous **jackdaw** is as good for digging up a worm as for piercing an egg.

Glossary

•BERRY
Small fruit with flesh surrounding the seeds or pips.

•BREEDING PLUMAGE
Birds put on breeding colours when they are pairing off. The plumage is often brighter than in winter.

•CARNIVORE
Animal feeding exclusively on meat. It hunts other animals for food. Foxes and beech martens, which live in towns, are carnivorous.

•CHRYSALIS
Hard case inside which a caterpillar turns into a butterfly or a moth.

•CONE
Woody structure, with scales, holding the seeds of pines and other conifers.

•DIAGNOSTIC FEATURE
Detail which, in combination with others, leads to the identification of an animal or plant.

•FRY
Very young fish. Fry are caught by many predators.

•HERBIVOROUS
Describes an animal which only eats plants.

•LARVA
The stage in an insect's life between the egg and the pupa or chrysalis. Caterpillars are larvae.

•NECTAR
Sugary liquid produced by flowers. Sought after by many insects.

•OMNIVOROUS
Describes an animal which eats several types of food, of both plant and animal origin.

•PASSERINE
Small sparrow-shaped birds characterised by a well-developed song. Examples of passerines are: sparrows, blackbirds, robins and warblers. Crows are the largest passerines. Often called song birds.

•PELLETS
Balls containing a mixture of fur and bones disgorged by raptors as they digest their food. They are the inedible parts of the prey. Fur and bits of bone from small mammals are found in them.

•PRIMARY FEATHERS
Main flight feathers attached to the outer half of the wing.

•PREDATOR
An animal which hunts live prey for food.

•RAPTOR
A bird of prey.

•RODENTS
The most numerous mammals on earth. Rats and mice come in to this category.

•ROOSTS
Where many birds congregate together to spend the night, seeking safety in numbers. Often in trees.

•RUMP
Lower part of a bird's back.

•SONAR
Describes a system for locating where

something is. It works by receiving the echo of a signal. Submarines, bats and dolphins find their way about by using their sonar system.

•TALONS
The powerful 'fingers' with sharp claws possessed by raptors.

•WING-COVERTS
The feathers which cover the forepart of the upper side of the wing.

•WING SPAN
Distance between the wing tips of an insect or bird.

Further reading

Burton J, *Collins Gem Wild Animals Photoguide*, HarperCollins, London, 1996
Chinery M, *Collins Pocket Guide Insects of Britain and Western Europe*, HarperCollins, London, 1986
Chinery M & Teagle W G, *Wildlife in Towns and Cities*, Country Life
Hofmann H, *Collins Nature Guide Wild Animals*, HarperCollins, London, 1995
Nicolai J, Singer D & Wothe K, *Collins Nature Guide Birds*, HarperCollins, London, 1994
Shirley P, *Urban Wildlife*, Whittet Books, 1990
Still, J *Collins Wild Guide Butterflies and Moths*, HarperCollins, London, 1996

Addresses

Royal Society for the Protection of Birds
The Lodge
Sandy
Bedfordshire SG19 2DL

Young Ornithologists Club
The youth branch of the RSPB (above).

Urban Wildlife Groups
The Wildlife Trust
The Green
Witham Park
Waterside South
Lincoln LN5 7JR

Index

Photographic credits

8 Michel et Christine Denis-Huot/ BIOS
12 Dominique Robert/Le Danube vert
17 Guilhem Lesaffre
19, **21**, **22** Dominique Robert /Le Danube vert
25 Bruce Coleman
33 Jean-Marie Prévot /BIOS